DeltaScience

Finding the Moon

CONTENTS

Think About . . .

People in Science

Did You Know?

What Do We See in the Sky?

We may see clouds.

We may see the **Sun.**

We may see stars.
We may see the **Moon.**

Why Does the Moon Shine?

The Moon has no light of its own. The Sun shines on the Moon. The light from the Sun **reflects** off the Moon. Then we can see the Moon shine.

What Are Moon Phases?

We look at the Moon. We can see different shapes. We call these shapes the **phases** of the Moon.

Some nights we can not see the Moon. But the Moon is still there. We call this the **new Moon.**

Some nights we can see a little bit of the Moon.

Some nights we can see more of the Moon.

Some nights the Moon looks like a ball or a circle. We call this the **full Moon.**

What Is the Moon Like?

The Moon has no air.

The Moon has mountains.

The Moon has big holes. The big holes are called **craters.** The craters were made by rocks that hit the Moon.

The Moon has dark, flat places. We call these places **seas.** But the seas on the Moon do not have water.

Neil Armstrong

Neil Armstrong was an **astronaut.** He was the first person to walk on the Moon. He collected Moon rocks for scientists to study.

Did You Know?

About the Size of the Moon

The Moon is smaller than **Earth.**
The Moon is smaller than the Sun.
But the Moon is much closer to Earth.
That is why the Moon looks big.

Glossary

astronaut someone who travels in space

crater a hole made by a rock that hit the Moon

Earth the planet we live on

full Moon the phase of the Moon when it looks like a ball or a circle

Moon a giant rock that travels around Earth

new Moon the phase of the Moon when we can not see it

phases the shapes of the Moon we see

reflect to bounce off of

seas dark flat places on the Moon with no water

Sun the star that gives us light and heat